ORLANDO
MAGIC

by Drew Silverman

Editor: Chrös McDougall
Copy Editor: Anna Comstock
Series design: Christa Schneider
Cover production: Marie Tupy
Interior production: Carol Castro

Photo Credits: John Raoux/AP Images, cover, 44; Peter Cosgrove/AP Images, 1, 24, 29, 30, 43 (middle); Steve Simoneau/AP Images, 4, 42 (bottom); Don Ryan/AP Images, 7, 42 (middle); Chris O'Meara/AP Images, 9, 15, 21, 23, 43 (top); Elaine Thompson/AP Images, 10; Marc Pesetsky/AP Images, 12; Nathaniel S. Butler/NBAE/Getty Images, 17, 42 (top); Stephan Savoia/AP Images, 18; Don Frazier/AP Images, 26; Yam Y. Huh/AP Images, 33; Kathy Willens/AP Images, 34; Eric Gay/AP Images, 36; Lance Murphey/AP Images, 39; Larry W. Smith/AP Images, 41, 43 (bottom); Scott A. Miller/AP Images, 47

Library of Congress Cataloging-in-Publication Data
Silverman, Drew, 1982-
  Orlando Magic / by Drew Silverman.
    p. cm. -- (Inside the NBA)
  Includes index.
  ISBN 978-1-61783-170-6
  1. Orlando Magic (Basketball team)--History--Juvenile literature. I. Title.
  GV885.52.O75S55 2012
  796.323'640975924--dc23
                          2011021687

TABLE OF CONTENTS

CHAPTER 1

HITTING THE JACKPOT

Shaquille O'Neal could not help but smile. Things were good. He was just 23 years old. His team, the Orlando Magic, was in just its sixth season of existence. Yet O'Neal and his Magic teammates were already heading to the National Basketball Association (NBA) Finals.

"When it comes time to play in big games, we always play well," O'Neal said that day in June 1995. "We proved that again."

The Magic had just defeated the Indiana Pacers 105–81 in the deciding Game 7 of the Eastern Conference finals. O'Neal had scored 25 points. To many, it was stunning to watch the young Magic defeat the veteran Pacers in such an important game.

"They certainly met the challenge tonight with flying colors," Pacers coach Larry Brown said. "I don't know when

Magic center Shaquille O'Neal goes up for a basket during the second round of the 1995 postseason. O'Neal led Orlando to the NBA Finals.

I've ever seen a team play a better game in an important game like they did."

The Magic's surprising run to the top of the Eastern Conference began in 1992. After each season, all of the teams that miss the playoffs enter a lottery that determines the top pick in that year's NBA Draft. The teams with the worst records have better chances of getting picked. In 1992, the Magic had a 15 percent chance of getting the number one pick. But they got it. And there was no question about whom they were going to draft.

O'Neal was universally considered the best player available. The 7-foot-1 center weighed more than 300 pounds. He was big, strong, and talented. He had averaged 24 points and 14 rebounds per game during his final season at Louisiana State University. The pick was viewed as a no-brainer. So, the Magic made it official on June 24, 1992. They chose O'Neal with the first pick in the draft. And their team was never the same again.

"I will be a force in the pros," O'Neal told *Sports Illustrated* prior to the draft lottery. "There are only a few players

Shaquille O'Neal waves to the crowd at the 1992 NBA Draft moments after the Orlando Magic selected him with the first pick.

who can dominate games, and I intend to be one of those players. I will be a force."

He lived up to his word. O'Neal was named the league's Rookie of the Year in 1992–93. He became the first rookie to make the All-Star Game since Michael Jordan of the Chicago Bulls did it in 1984–85. And he helped the Magic win 41 games.

Orlando had only won 21 games the season before O'Neal arrived.

The good fortune was just beginning for the Magic. They entered the 1993 NBA Draft lottery with only a 1.5 percent chance of getting the first pick. But they won it again!

With the first pick, Orlando chose Chris Webber, a talented

SHAQ THE STAR

Shaquille O'Neal initially became famous for his size and power on the basketball court. He later became well known for his acting and music off the basketball court. But he also became popular for his nicknames over the years. By some accounts, O'Neal has had 20 or more nicknames throughout his career. Some of the more common ones are "The Diesel," "Shaq Daddy," and "The Big Daddy."

O'Neal's popularity reached the national level on January 21, 1991. The then-college sophomore was on the cover of *Sports Illustrated* for the first time. But it certainly was not the last. Through May 2010, O'Neal had been on the cover of *Sports Illustrated* 16 times. Only seven athletes had ever graced the cover more: Basketball stars Michael Jordan (49 times), Magic Johnson (23), Kareem Abdul-Jabbar (22), and Larry Bird (17); boxing legend Muhammad Ali (38); and golf icons Jack Nicklaus (22) and Tiger Woods (19).

power forward from the University of Michigan. But they immediately traded Webber to the Golden State Warriors for fellow rookie point guard Anfernee "Penny" Hardaway.

In their first season together, 1993–94, O'Neal and Hardaway led the Magic to 50 wins. The team finished second in the Atlantic Division. And for the first time in its history, Orlando made the playoffs. However, the more experienced Pacers eliminated the Magic in the first round of the postseason.

O'Neal and Hardaway were only 22 years old. Even the team's veterans, Dennis Scott and Nick Anderson, were only 25 and 26, respectively. So that off-season, the Magic signed Horace Grant as a free agent. Grant was an All-Star forward who had won three NBA championships with

Magic point guard Anfernee "Penny" Hardaway puts up a shot after being tripped during a 1995 playoff game.

the Chicago Bulls. He brought experience and toughness to Orlando.

With a new starting lineup that featured O'Neal, Hardaway, and Grant, the Magic became a force during the 1994–95 season. They won 15 of their first 18 games and finished with a 57–25 record. Orlando won the Atlantic Division for

the first time and earned the top seed in the Eastern Conference playoffs.

In addition to team success, Grant's arrival also brought out the best in O'Neal. He led the league in scoring with 29.3 points per game. He also ranked in the NBA's top 10 in rebounding, blocked shots, and field-goal percentage.

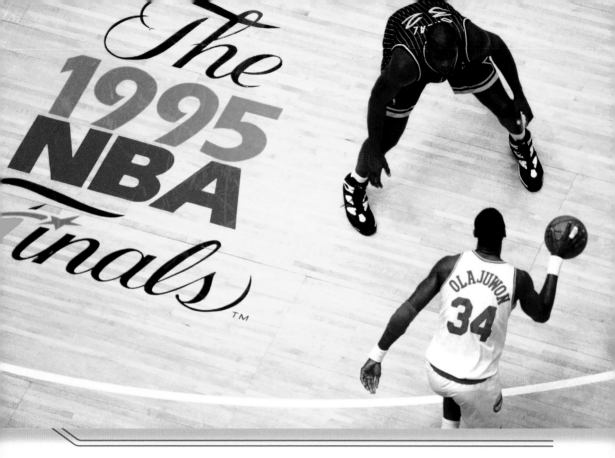

The Magic's Shaquille O'Neal guards the Houston Rockets' Hakeem Olajuwon during the 1995 NBA Finals. The Rockets won in four games.

"No predictions," Grant said when he signed with the Magic. "But I'll guarantee this: We won't lose in the first round."

Grant proved to be a man of his word. Orlando opened the playoffs with a 47-point win over the Boston Celtics. The Magic eventually won the series, three games to one.

The next series matched the Magic against Jordan and the Bulls. Many consider Jordan to be the best player ever. But he had just returned from retirement, and his Bulls could not handle the upstart Magic.

Orlando won the series in six games. O'Neal averaged 24.3 points per game. But it was

Anderson who hit the series-winning shot—a jumper with 43 seconds left in Game 6. The Magic outscored the Bulls 14–0 in the final three minutes that night. Next came the Pacers in the conference finals.

This series was tighter. O'Neal, Grant, and Hardaway all had double-doubles in Orlando's 105–101 win in Game 1.

A double-double is when a player records double digits in two statistics in one game. In Game 2, O'Neal made 15 of his 21 shots and finished with 39 points in a 119–114 Magic win. However, Orlando lost three of the next four games, including Game 4 at the buzzer. That set up the important Game 7 victory that had O'Neal smiling.

Despite O'Neal's statement after the Game 7 victory, the Magic's dream run ended short of an NBA championship. Facing star center Hakeem Olajuwon and the Houston Rockets in the NBA Finals, Orlando lost all four games.

The Rockets won their second straight title, but the Magic gained valuable experience along the way. With a young core returning, Magic fans hoped the 1994–95 season was just the start of something big.

CHAPTER 2

THE MAGIC BEGINS

The mid-1980s were an exciting time for basketball fans in Florida. The NBA had planned to add an expansion franchise in either Orlando or Miami. But when ownership groups in both cities made enticing proposals, the league decided to give teams to both of them.

The Miami Heat began play during the 1988–89 season along with the Charlotte Hornets, another expansion team. The following year, in 1989–90, the Magic officially joined the NBA along with the Minnesota Timberwolves.

The first coach of the Magic was Matt Guokas. He had spent the previous seven seasons with

What's in a Name?

One of the first things Orlando had to do upon getting an expansion NBA team was pick a nickname. So, the Orlando Sentinel held a contest where fans could suggest names for the team. More than 4,000 names were suggested, but the final candidates were the Heat, the Tropics, the Juice, and the Magic. Ultimately, team officials chose the Magic, while the expansion team in Miami ended up taking the Heat.

The Magic's Sam Vincent defends against the Miami Heat's Sherman Douglas during a 1989 game. The Heat joined the NBA in 1988–89 and the Magic joined in 1989–90.

the Philadelphia 76ers. He was an assistant coach for four of those years, and the head coach for the last three.

Coach Guokas and general manager Pat Williams oversaw the Magic's expansion draft on June 15, 1989. The expansion draft allowed the expansion teams to select unprotected players from NBA's existing teams. Orlando chose 12 players that day. One, guard Reggie

Theus from the Atlanta Hawks, had been an All-Star. Another, Scott Skiles from the Indiana Pacers, would become the Magic's starting point guard.

Later that month, the Magic participated in their first NBA Draft. With the 11th overall pick, they chose guard/forward Nick Anderson from the University of Illinois.

Most expansion teams struggle during their first few seasons. The Magic were no exception. They got off to a solid start in 1989–90, winning seven of their first 14 games. But then they only won 11 of their final 68 games to finish in last place in the Central Division.

The next season, 1990–91, the Magic moved to the Midwest Division and improved their win total from 18 to 31. It was the largest win improvement of any NBA team that season. One Orlando player who greatly

Magic point guard Scott Skiles dribbles around a Golden State Warriors defender while a teammate sets a pick in 1993.

improved during the season was Skiles. The 6-foot-1 point guard led the Magic in points (17.2 per game) and assists (8.4). He was named the NBA's Most Improved Player.

During a December game against the Denver Nuggets, Skiles set the NBA record for assists in a game. He dished out 30 assists in a 155–116 victory. "Someday, someone will get 31," Skiles said years later, "so I don't think too much about the assists record. But I am proud to know that of all the great playmakers . . . I have more assists than any of them in one game."

Orlando finished the season with 20 wins and 18 losses over the last three months. Things were looking up for the second-year team.

NICK ANDERSON

The Magic selected forward/ guard Nick Anderson from the University of Illinois with the 11th pick in the 1989 NBA Draft. He went on to become one of Orlando's first iconic players. Anderson averaged double-figure points in all 10 of his seasons with the Magic, from 1989–90 to 1998–99. Through the 2010–11 season, he held the Magic career records for games played (692), minutes played (22,440), points (10,650), steals (1,004), field goals made (4,075), field goals attempted (8,976), and three-pointers attempted (2,480). He also ranked in the top five in Magic history in rebounds, assists, and blocks.

However, as of 2010–11, the team has not retired his No. 25 jersey—or any other player's jersey, for that matter. In 2010, the *Orlando Sentinel* asked Anderson if he had given up hope that his jersey would ever be retired. "I have," he said. "I don't think it will be done."

Another bright spot was the play of rookie forward Dennis Scott. The sharp-shooter out of Georgia Tech was the fourth pick in the 1990 draft. And he made an immediate contribution. Scott's 125 three-pointers in 1990–91 were the most by a rookie in league history.

In addition to Skiles and Scott, four other Magic players averaged at least 12 points per game in 1990–91. Veteran forward Terry Catledge averaged 14.6 points per game, while Anderson chipped in 14.1 points per game. Guard/forward Otis Smith scored 13.9 points per game, and sixth man Jerry Reynolds came in at 12.9 points per game.

Skiles racked up the assists again in 1991–92, averaging 7.3 per game. Anderson and Scott each set a career high with 19.9 points per

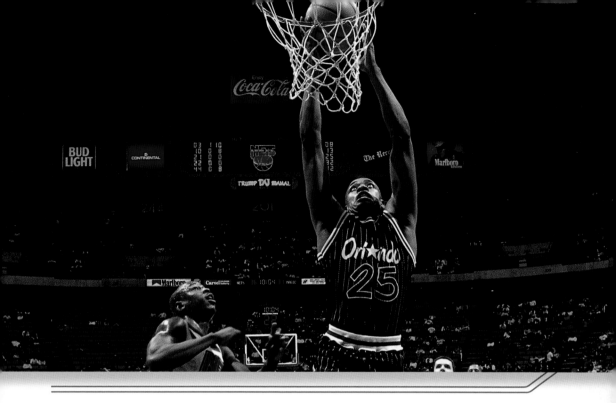

The Magic's Nick Anderson dunks against the New Jersey Nets during a 1991 game. Anderson played for the Magic for the team's first 10 seasons.

game. But the team victories did not come so easily. Scott missed more than 60 games due to a leg injury. And Anderson sat out 21 games with a broken right eye socket. Other key Magic players, such as guards Sam Vincent and Anthony Bowie, missed time with injuries, as well.

The Magic won just 21 games that year. They finished with the second-worst record in the NBA. That meant Orlando would have the second-best chance to get the first pick in that year's draft lottery.

Still, the odds that they would win it were just 15 percent. But when the lottery was over, Orlando had magically won the number one pick. With it, they would take a transformational player.

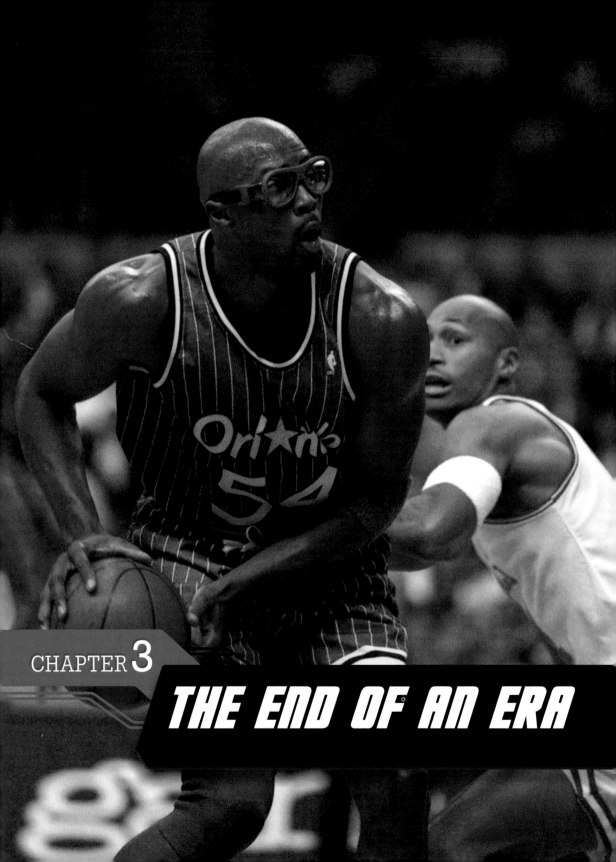

CHAPTER 3

THE END OF AN ERA

After adding center Shaquille O'Neal during the 1992 draft, the Magic enjoyed an immediate rise in popularity and victories, capped by their trip to the NBA Finals in 1995. However, that turned out to be the highlight of O'Neal's time in Orlando.

O'Neal broke his thumb during a preseason game the next season, 1995–96. That caused him to miss the Magic's first 22 games. Even so, he still averaged 26.6 points and 11 rebounds per game to lead the team in both categories for the season. Anfernee "Penny" Hardaway chipped in 21.7 points per game, while Dennis Scott (17.5), Nick Anderson (14.7), and Horace Grant (13.4) also averaged in double figures.

In the regular season, the Magic overcame O'Neal's injury to win 60 games. It was Orlando's only 60-win season through

Forward Horace Grant averaged 13.4 points, 9.2 rebounds, and 1.2 blocks per game to help the Magic win a franchise-record 60 games in 1995–96.

AFTER SHAQ

The day Shaquille O'Neal signed with the Los Angeles Lakers was a tough one for everyone associated with the Magic. "It took me 10 years to halfway get over it," said general manager Pat Williams, who had been with the Magic since before their inaugural season of 1989–90. "To lose a 24-year-old that is the franchise is just very, very painful."

"I'll always remember that day," Magic guard Nick Anderson said. "I was watching the Olympics and there was a bulletin that flashed across the screen, and then there was [Lakers general manager] Jerry West holding up a Shaquille O'Neal jersey. And then my dad called me and said, 'The championship just went to L.A.'"

Ultimately, O'Neal won three titles with the Lakers. He later won a fourth with the Miami Heat. "We were the team of the future," Williams said. "We had a solid nucleus. I don't think anybody saw it coming."

2010–11. They won the Atlantic Division by 13 games over the New York Knicks. But everyone knew that the real test would come in the Eastern Conference finals against the Chicago Bulls.

Led by the NBA's Most Valuable Player (MVP), Michael Jordan, the Bulls had won a league-record 72 games during the regular season. And the Magic proved to be no match for Chicago, losing all four games in the series. Their Game 4 loss, a 106–101 defeat, would be the last game O'Neal ever played for the Magic.

"He'll be a great player . . . someday," Bulls forward Dennis Rodman said of O'Neal. "But if he wants to go home with a trophy, he better learn how to win."

Eventually, O'Neal did learn how to win. And he did go home with several

A healthy Shaquille O'Neal led the Magic past the Detroit Pistons in the first round of the 1996 playoffs. Orlando eventually lost to the Chicago Bulls in the conference finals.

championship trophies. But none of them came for Orlando.

In the summer of 1996, the Los Angeles Lakers were making a very hard push for O'Neal, who was a free agent for the first time. O'Neal enjoyed life in Orlando, but his acting and rapping aspirations made Los Angeles a logical landing spot. On July 18, 1996, O'Neal made it official. He signed a seven-year, $121 million contract with the Lakers.

O'Neal's departure left the Magic in a tough spot. They

were coming off a 60-win season and still had plenty of talent in place. But there was now a big hole in the middle.

"I'm not going to tell you we can still win a championship, because I just don't know," said a dejected Hardaway. "This is bad."

Despite losing O'Neal, the Magic had a solid 1996–97 season. They went 45–37 and made the playoffs, but lost to the Miami Heat in the first round.

From an individual standpoint, Hardaway took over as the team's primary scoring option that season. He led Orlando with 20.5 points and 5.6 assists per game

In an effort to replace O'Neal's void, the Magic traded for veteran center Rony Seikaly. He averaged a career-high 17.3

Penny

For a time during the 1990s, Anfernee "Penny" Hardaway was one of the most popular players in the NBA. He had the catchy nickname. He owned several endorsement deals. And he was a flashy player on a winning team. But fans in Orlando were slow to warm up to Hardaway. Many Magic fans had wanted the team to keep Chris Webber, whom they drafted in 1993 and then traded for Hardaway.

points per game, to go along with 9.5 rebounds per game, during the 1996–97 season.

"Our best acquisition ever," said Magic assistant coach Richie Adubato.

Brian Hill, who had coached Orlando to the 1995 NBA Finals, had been fired shortly after the 1997 All-Star Game that year. Adubato was promoted to head coach. He guided Orlando to a 21–12

Point guard Anfernee "Penny" Hardaway led the Magic to a 45–37 record in 1996–97, but they lost to the Miami Heat in the playoffs' first round.

Magic point guard Darrell Armstrong averaged 13.8 points, 6.7 assists, and 2.2 steals off the bench en route to winning the NBA's Sixth Man of the Year Award in 1998–99.

record the rest of the way, but he would not return the following season.

The Magic opted instead to bring in Chuck Daly. Already a Hall of Fame coach, Daly had led the Detroit Pistons to NBA titles in 1989 and 1990. He also had coached the 1992 US Olympic team, known as the "Dream Team," to the gold medal in Barcelona, Spain.

Daly went on to coach the Magic for the next two seasons.

A Winning Coach

On March 27, 1998, Magic coach Chuck Daly recorded his 600th career victory. With a 100–75 win over the Houston Rockets, Daly became the 15th coach in NBA history to reach that milestone. Through 2010–11, he is the fifth-fastest coach in NBA history to get to 600 wins. The only coaches who had gotten there faster were Pat Riley, Red Auerbach, Jerry Sloan, and Don Nelson.

In 1997–98, the team missed the playoffs. It went 41–41 that season while fighting through numerous injuries. Hardaway missed 63 games with leg injuries. Anderson missed 15 games with a broken hand. And Seikaly played in just 47 games before he was traded to the New Jersey Nets.

Hardaway got healthy in 1998–99, playing in all 50 games during the lockout-shortened season. He averaged 15.8 points per game and paced a balanced scoring attack. Anderson chipped in with 14.9 points per game, while point guard Darrell Armstrong burst onto the scene to average 13.8 points per game. He was named the NBA's Sixth Man of the Year, as well as the league's Most Improved Player.

Orlando made it to the playoffs. However, it was another brief postseason run for the Magic. The Philadelphia 76ers upset the Magic in the first round. That off-season, the team traded Hardaway to the Phoenix Suns. Anderson was traded to the Sacramento Kings. And Daly announced his retirement from coaching.

"None of us expected the number of changes we ended up making," said Magic general manager John Gabriel. But those changes were only just beginning.

CHAPTER **4**

A PLAN
GONE AWRY

The 1999–2000 season was a pleasant surprise for the Magic. The team fielded a roster that was not expected to contend for the playoffs. Penny Hardaway was gone. Nick Anderson and Horace Grant were gone. And Shaquille O'Neal was long gone.

But in stepped a new leader on the court and a new leader on the sidelines. Darrell Armstrong, a feisty 6-foot point guard, became the team's top scorer. And on the bench, Glenn "Doc" Rivers took over as head coach.

Rivers was a respected leader from his days as an NBA point guard. However, this was his first head coaching job. Some people doubted the hire by general manager John Gabriel. But those doubts quieted quickly when Rivers led

The Magic's Darrell Armstrong goes for a basket during a 2000 game against the Chicago Bulls. He averaged career highs in points and steals in 1999–2000.

the Magic to a 41–41 record and was named Coach of the Year.

Meanwhile, Armstrong led the Magic in points, assists, steals, and minutes played. Yet, Gabriel knew that he needed more help.

So during the 2000 off-season, Orlando signed two of the biggest free agents available. Shooting guard Tracy McGrady and small forward Grant Hill signed identical seven-year, $93 million contracts. McGrady was considered a rising star, while

Hill was an established veteran. He had already played in five All-Star Games for the Detroit Pistons. Together, the expectations were that McGrady and Hill would turn the Magic back into title contenders.

Needless to say, the plan did not work. During the four seasons Hill and McGrady spent together, the Magic won a total of only five playoff games. And they never won more than 44 games in any regular season. One of the big reasons was Hill's injuries.

In his first season with Orlando, Hill had an ankle injury that limited him to playing in only four games. However, that injury opened the door for McGrady to shine. The 21-year-old averaged 26.8 points per game. That was 11 more than he had averaged for the Toronto Raptors the year before. McGrady led the team in

The Magic signed Tracy McGrady, *left*, and Grant Hill in 2000 with the hope that the two stars would lead the team back to the NBA Finals.

scoring and finished second in rebounding, assists, blocks, and steals. He also made his first All-Star team and earned the NBA's Most Improved Player Award. Still, the Milwaukee Bucks eliminated the Magic in the first round of the playoffs.

When he joined the Magic, Hill called McGrady "the best player in the game." Prior to the 2001–02 season, an opposing scout told *Sports Illustrated*, "Tracy McGrady is the best player in the East. . . . All Hill has to do is fit in."

Magic swingman Tracy McGrady drives to the hoop during a 2002 game against the New Jersey Nets.

But again, things did not go according to plan. Hill once again struggled with injuries during the 2001–02 season. Another ankle ailment caused the forward to miss 68 games. But for the second straight year, McGrady stepped up in Hill's absence.

McGrady, who was also known as "T-Mac," finished fourth in the NBA with 25.6 points per game. He was named to the All-NBA first team and finished fourth in MVP voting. McGrady and Los Angeles Lakers star Kobe Bryant were the only players in the NBA to average at least 25 points, 5 rebounds, and 5 assists per game in 2001–02.

Armstrong had a solid season, averaging 12.4 points per game and leading the team with 5.5 assists and 1.9 steals per game. Also chipping in during Hill's latest absence was second-year forward Mike Miller. He averaged 15.2 points per game and gave Orlando a dangerous three-point threat. The team had other capable shooters in Pat Garrity and Troy Hudson, as well.

The Magic's average of 100.5 points per game was the fourth best in the NBA. Their offense carried them into the postseason. However, they lost in the opening round for the second straight year.

Early in the 2002–03 season, Hill proclaimed himself as dangerous as ever. "My goal is to come back better than before,"

Calling the Hall

Prior to the 2001–02 season, the Magic signed veteran center Patrick Ewing. The 11-time All-Star spent one season with Orlando, averaging six points and four rebounds in 13.9 minutes per game. Ewing went on to reach the Hall of Fame, becoming one of two former Magic players to be enshrined there. The other is forward Dominique Wilkins, who played in 27 games for Orlando during the 1998–99 season, averaging 5 points and 2.6 rebounds in 9.3 minutes per game.

he said. "I have a long way to go, but I think I can be as good as anybody in this league."

However, it would be another lost season for the injury-prone star. He played in just 29 games, bringing his three-year total to 47 games played.

McGrady, meanwhile, took the leap to superstardom. Now 23 years old, he led the NBA with 32.1 points per game. He also averaged career highs

T-MAC

Tracy McGrady holds many Magic records, including the mark for most points in a game. On March 10, 2004, McGrady scored 62 points against the Washington Wizards. He was just the fourth NBA player in the previous 12 years to score 60 points in a game, joining Michael Jordan, David Robinson, and Shaquille O'Neal.

Through 2010–11, McGrady is one of 16 players in NBA history to win multiple scoring titles in his career. And he is one of just 12 players to win back-to-back scoring titles. On February 2, 2004, McGrady became the second-youngest player in NBA history to reach 10,000 points, trailing only Kobe Bryant. However, LeBron James has since passed both of them. From 2000–01 to 2006–07, McGrady made seven consecutive All-Star teams. He was named to the All-NBA first team twice—in 2001–02 and 2002–03. He also made the All-NBA second team three times and the third team twice.

of 5.5 assists and 1.7 steals per game. For the second straight season, he finished fourth in MVP voting.

Still, the Magic could not help but wonder: What if Hill had been healthy? "I don't know how Grant can come back," McGrady admitted. "But he's fighting, and I'm not giving up on him."

Even without Hill, the Magic finished with a .500 or better record for the 11th straight season. They made the playoffs with a 42–40 record as the eighth seed.

In their first-round series against the top-seeded Detroit Pistons, the Magic jumped out to a three-games-to-one lead. But Orlando then lost the next three games, including a 15-point loss in Game 7, which cost them the series. "This is the worst of them all," McGrady said.

The Magic's Tracy McGrady controls the ball against Los Angeles Lakers defender Kobe Bryant during a 2004 game.

Things did not improve for Orlando during the 2003–04 season. The Magic won only 21 games, matching the second-fewest wins in franchise history. They won their season opener against the New York Knicks, but then lost their next 19 games. Hill missed the entire season and Garrity played in only two games. Orlando finished the season with the worst record in the NBA. But for the third time in team history, a little bit of lottery luck was right around the corner.

CHAPTER 5

IT'S SUPERMAN!

Following the nightmare 2003–04 season, the Magic became the first team to win the draft lottery three times. After drafting Shaquille O'Neal in 1992 and Chris Webber—who was then traded for Anfernee Hardaway—in 1993, the Magic went for another big guy in 2004.

This time, it was Dwight Howard. A 6-foot-11 center, Howard was entering the draft straight out of high school. He was just 18 years old, but his potential was too much for the Magic to pass up. Still, the NBA proved to be a transition for the muscular big man.

"In high school, Dwight could just turn around and shoot over guys," said Magic coach Johnny Davis, who replaced Doc Rivers during the 2003–04 season. "Now he's gone from the kiddie pool to the adult pool."

In his first season, Howard averaged 12 points and 10 rebounds per game. Fellow rookie Jameer Nelson, a point guard, averaged 8.7 points and 3 assists per game. But they

Dwight Howard addresses the media after the Magic made him the number one pick in the 2004 NBA Draft.

Magic star Dwight Howard soars toward the hoop wearing his Superman costume during the 2008 Slam Dunk Contest.

were hardly the only new faces on the Magic roster.

Before that season, new general manager John Weisbrod traded superstar Tracy McGrady and three others to the Houston Rockets for a package of players that included All-Star guard Steve Francis. Orlando also brought in forward Hedo Turkoglu and later acquired another veteran, shooting guard Doug Christie. And Grant Hill finally stayed healthy, for the most part, playing in 67 games. "We needed to start fresh," said Weisbrod.

The Magic still struggled in 2004–05. With 18 games remaining, Weisbrod fired Davis. The team finished 36–46 under coach Chris Jent.

The next coach of the team was a familiar face. Brian Hill had coached the Magic from 1994 to 1997. He returned to guide the team at the start of the 2005–06 season. But Orlando finished 36–46 for the second straight season and missed the playoffs for the third consecutive year.

The Magic returned to the postseason in 2006–07. However, the Detroit Pistons swept them in the first round. Still, Howard became an All-Star for the first time that season. He averaged 17.6 points and 12.3 rebounds per game.

Grant Hill was somewhat healthy for the second time in the previous three years. He played in 65 games. But his contract expired at the end of the season, and he was not re-signed. In addition, Brian Hill would not return as head coach for the 2007–08 season.

SUPERMAN

In 2008, Dwight Howard created a buzz at All-Star weekend when he became the tallest player to ever win the Slam Dunk Contest. The 6-foot-11 Howard played to his nickname, Superman, by wearing a red cape with an "S" on the chest. He received a perfect score from the judges for each of his first two dunks. In the final round, both of his slams drew immense applause from the crowd.

"I think the dunk contest is back," said Howard, who is known for his fun, joking personality. "I don't think people want to see the same old dunks. They want to see something else, see some spice."

It wasn't just the fans who were impressed. "We watched him work on it after practice," said Magic teammate Rashard Lewis. "None of us had any idea about the suit and cape, though. When he pulled his jersey off and had that on, I almost fell off my couch. That guy's crazy."

Backing Out

On May 31, 2007, after Brian Hill's departure, Billy Donovan was named head coach of the Magic. Donovan had just won back-to-back national championships at the University of Florida. He agreed to a five-year, $27.5 million contract and was introduced in a formal press conference. But just three days later, Donovan pulled out of the deal, claiming that his heart was still at Florida. On June 5, Donovan and the Magic agreed to terminate the contract. That same day, Orlando extended an offer to Stan Van Gundy, who accepted the deal to become the Magic's new head coach.

Former Miami Heat coach Stan Van Gundy replaced him. The Magic also traded for sharp-shooting forward Rashard Lewis that off-season.

"We set out at the start of free agency to get a big-time player, someone who could score the basketball," general manager Otis Smith said. "We targeted that guy and we got that guy."

Together, Howard and Lewis shined in their first season together. Howard averaged 20.7 points per game and was named the starting center for the Eastern Conference All-Star team. Lewis made a career-high 226 three-pointers and averaged 18.2 points per game. And Turkoglu, with 19.5 points per game, was named the NBA's Most Improved Player.

The Magic finished the 2007–08 season 52–30 and won their division outright for the first time since 1995–96. Then they dispatched of the Toronto Raptors in the first round of the postseason. It was their first playoff series win since 1995–96. However, Orlando was no match for the Pistons in the second round, losing that series in five games.

In 2008–09, the Magic became a legitimate title contender. They finished 59–23,

Magic forward Rashard Lewis led the NBA with 220 three-pointers made during the 2008–09 season.

the second-most wins in team history. They won the Southeast Division for a second straight year. Howard led the league in rebounding and blocks, and he was named Defensive Player of the Year.

In the first round of the playoffs, the Magic disposed of the Philadelphia 76ers. The next round brought the defending champion Boston Celtics. The Celtics took a 3–2 series lead, but Orlando won the last two games, including a 101–82 victory in Boston in Game 7. Turkoglu led the way that night with 25 points. Howard had 12 points, 16 rebounds, and five blocks.

Orlando carried its magic into the conference finals against the Cleveland Cavaliers. The Magic lost a heartbreaker in Game 2 when Cavaliers star LeBron James hit a three-pointer at the buzzer to win the game. But Orlando battled back to win the series four games to two.

Howard had a dominant performance in Game 6 against Cleveland. He scored 40 points and pulled down 14 rebounds. Thanks to his effort, the Magic were heading back to the NBA Finals for the first time in 14 years.

"For us as a team, we understand how everybody has talked about us for the last couple of years," Howard said. "We can beat anybody."

The Magic were no match for Kobe Bryant and the Los Angeles Lakers in the NBA Finals, though. Orlando was able to keep the games close—two went into overtime. But the Lakers won the championship four games to one.

"It hurts," Howard said after Game 5. "It hurts a lot.

But you can learn a lot from losing. Sometimes you've got to lose to win."

Behind the maturing Howard and the recently acquired forward Vince Carter, the Magic returned to the Eastern Conference finals in 2009–10. But the Celtics beat them in six games.

With the NBA's balance of power shifting to the Eastern Conference, the Magic made some moves to try to remain among the elite. Early in the 2010–11 season, they traded Lewis to the Washington Wizards for three-time All-Star guard Gilbert Arenas. That same day, they dealt Carter, an

Magic point guard Jameer Nelson goes up for a basket against the Los Angeles Lakers during the 2009 NBA Finals.

eight-time All-Star, to the Phoenix Suns. In return for Carter, a future first-round draft pick, and two other players, Orlando received former Magic forward Turkoglu, as well as veteran guard Jason Richardson and young forward Earl Clark.

The trades helped the Magic remain one of the better teams in the NBA. They entered the playoffs as the fourth seed in the Eastern Conference. However, the fifth-seeded Atlanta Hawks upset the Magic in six games in the first round.

It was a frustrating end to the season, but with a young superstar in Dwight Howard leading the way, the Magic look to be closer to winning their first NBA title than another NBA Draft lottery.

TIMELINE

1989	The Magic select 12 players in the expansion draft on June 15, the most notable of which is point guard Scott Skiles.
1989	The Magic choose Nick Anderson with their first-ever selection in the NBA Draft on June 27.
1989	The Magic officially begin play in the NBA, joining the Minnesota Timberwolves as the league's twenty-sixth and twenty-seventh franchises, on November 4.
1990	Skiles sets the NBA record with 30 assists in a win over the Denver Nuggets on December 30.
1992	The Magic win the NBA Draft lottery and select Louisiana State University star Shaquille O'Neal with the first pick in the draft.
1993	After winning the lottery again, the Magic select Chris Webber with the first pick in the draft. He is later traded to the Golden State Warriors for Anfernee "Penny" Hardaway.
1994	The Magic's first trip to the postseason ends with a three-game sweep by the Indiana Pacers.
1995	The Magic defeat the Pacers in the Eastern Conference finals to reach their first NBA Finals. However, the Houston Rockets sweep them in the Finals.
1996	O'Neal signs as a free agent with the Los Angeles Lakers on July 18.

1999 The Magic trade Anderson, their longest-tenured player, to the Sacramento Kings on August 3.

1999 The Magic trade Hardaway to the Phoenix Suns on August 5.

2000 The Magic acquire Tracy McGrady in a sign-and-trade with the Toronto Raptors, and they acquire Grant Hill in a sign-and-trade with the Detroit Pistons.

2004 McGrady sets the Magic franchise record by scoring 62 points against the Washington Wizards on March 10.

2004 After winning the NBA Draft lottery for a third time, the Magic select Dwight Howard from Southwest Atlanta Christian Academy in Atlanta, Georgia.

2007 The Magic name Stan Van Gundy head coach on June 7.

2007 The Magic acquire Rashard Lewis in a sign-and-trade with the Seattle SuperSonics on July 11.

2009 The Magic defeat the Cleveland Cavaliers in the Eastern Conference finals to advance to the NBA Finals. However, they lose to the Los Angeles Lakers in the Finals.

2011 The Magic trade Lewis to the Washington Wizards for Gilbert Arenas. They also trade Vince Carter and two other players to the Suns for Hedo Turkoglu, Jason Richardson, and Earl Clark. However, the Atlanta Hawks upset the Magic in the playoffs' first round.

QUICK STATS

FRANCHISE HISTORY

Orlando Magic (1989–)

NBA FINALS

1995, 2009

CONFERENCE FINALS

1995, 1996, 2009, 2010

DIVISION CHAMPIONSHIPS

1995, 1996, 1999, 2008, 2009, 2010

KEY PLAYERS
(position[s]; seasons with team)

Nick Anderson (G/F; 1989–99)
Darrell Armstrong (G; 1995–2003)
Horace Grant (F; 1994–99, 2001–02)
Anfernee Hardaway (G; 1993–99)
Grant Hill (F; 2000–07)
Dwight Howard (C; 2004–)
Rashard Lewis (F; 2007–10)
Tracy McGrady (G/F; 2000–04)
Jameer Nelson (G; 2004–)
Shaquille O'Neal (C; 1992–96)
Dennis Scott (F; 1990–97)
Scott Skiles (G; 1989–94)
Hedo Turkoglu (F; 2004–09; 2010–)

KEY COACHES

Brian Hill (1993–97; 2005–07):
    267–192; 18–22 (postseason)
Doc Rivers (1999–2003):
    171–168; 5–10 (postseason)
Stan Van Gundy (2007–):
    222–106; 28–20 (postseason)

HOME ARENAS

Amway Arena (1989–2010)
Amway Center (2010–)

*All statistics through 2010–11 season

QUOTES AND ANECDOTES

"The impact of our first exhibition game was so enormous it really set the tone for the whole year." —Pat Williams, the Magic's first team president. Orlando had defeated the defending NBA champion Detroit Pistons in its first ever preseason game in 1989.

Anfernee Hardaway's mother used to call him "pretty" when he was very young. Because of her accent, this got confused with "Penny," which became Hardaway's nickname.

In the 1993 All-Star Game, Magic rookie Shaquille O'Neal was double- and triple-teamed by the Western Conference big men. They did not want O'Neal receiving any more of the spotlight than he already was.

"Pray for a hurricane." —Sacramento Kings coach Garry St. Jean in 1994, when asked how Shaquille O'Neal can be stopped

The sign-and-trade for Grant Hill was initially viewed as a great success for the Magic. But not only did Hill suffer through many injuries in Orlando, the Detroit Pistons received Ben Wallace in the trade. Wallace went on to become a four-time Defensive Player of the Year who helped Detroit win the NBA championship in 2004.

In 2008–09 and 2009–10, Dwight Howard became the first player in NBA history to lead the league in rebounds per game and blocks per game in consecutive seasons.

GLOSSARY

assist

A pass that leads directly to a made basket.

contender

A team that is in the race for a championship or playoff berth.

contract

A binding agreement about, for example, years of commitment by a basketball player in exchange for a given salary.

draft

A system used by professional sports leagues to select new players in order to spread incoming talent among all teams. The NBA Draft is held each June.

expansion

In sports, the addition of a franchise or franchises to a league.

franchise

An entire sports organization, including the players, coaches, and staff.

free agent

A player whose contract has expired and who is able to sign with a team of his choice.

general manager

The executive who is in charge of the team's overall operation. He or she hires and fires coaches, drafts players, and signs free agents.

lockout

When an employer prevents employees from working, usually due to a labor dispute.

postseason

The games in which the best teams play after the regular-season schedule has been completed.

rebound

To secure the basketball after a missed shot.

sixth man

A team's best player who is not in the starting lineup.

FOR MORE INFORMATION

Further Reading

Ballard, Chris. *The Art of a Beautiful Game: The Thinking Fan's Tour of the NBA*. New York: Simon & Schuster, 2009.

Simmons, Bill. *The Book of Basketball: The NBA According to the Sports Guy*. New York: Random House, 2009.

Williams, Pat. *Making Magic: How Orlando won an NBA team*. Orlando, Florida: Sentinel Communications, 1989.

Web Links

To learn more about the Orlando Magic, visit ABDO Publishing Company online at **www.abdopublishing.com**. Web sites about the Magic are featured on our Book Links page. These links are routinely monitored and updated to provide the most current information available.

Places to Visit

Amway Center
400 W Church St
Orlando, FL 32801
407-440-7000
www.amwaycenter.com
This has been the Magic's home arena since 2010. The team plays 41 regular-season games here each year. Tours are available when the Magic are not playing.

Florida Sports Hall of Fame
Lake Myrtle Sports Complex
905 Lake Myrtle Park Drive
Auburndale, FL 33823
863-551-4750
www.floridasportshalloffame.com
This museum provides many exhibits and memorabilia on the history of the Magic and Florida's other professional and collegiate sports teams.

Naismith Memorial Basketball Hall of Fame
1000 West Columbus Avenue
Springfield, MA 01105
413-781-6500
www.hoophall.com
This hall of fame and museum highlights the greatest players and moments in the history of basketball. Former Magic players Patrick Ewing and Dominique Wilkins are enshrined here.

INDEX

About the Author

Drew Silverman is a sportswriter based in Philadelphia, Pennsylvania. He graduated from Syracuse University in 2004. He then worked as a sportswriter and editor at ESPN's headquarters in Bristol, Connecticut, before returning home to Philadelphia. After several years as the sports editor for *The Bulletin* newspaper, he began working for *Comcast SportsNet* as a content manager. Drew has covered everything from college basketball to Major League Baseball and National Football League games to the Stanley Cup Finals.